Forward

This bulletin provides a basic understanding of the FCC regulations for low-power, unlicensed transmitters, followed by some answers to commonly-asked questions. To assist readers in locating specific rules, the rule references are displayed in a column to the right of the text.

We welcome comments on improvements that can be made to this bulletin. Please address such comments to:

Federal Communications Commission
Office of Engineering and Technology
Customer Service Branch, MS 1300F2
7435 Oakland Mills Road
Columbia, MD 21046
Fax: (301) 344-2050
E-Mail: labinfo@fcc.gov

Note: Editorial changes have been made in this bulletin to reflect changes in the cordless telephone frequencies, the names, addresses and telephone numbers of information sources and FCC offices. This bulletin does not contain information concerning personal communication services (PCS) transmitters operating under Part 15, Subpart D of the rules. The FCC rules and regulations governing PCS transmitters may be found in 47 CFR, Parts 0 to 19. This bulletin also does not cover recent changes in the rules to accomodate devices operating above 40 GHz (millimeter waves). These changes will be discussed in later editions of this bulletin.

The fees listed in this bulletin reflect those in effect at the time of printing, but are subject to change. Current fee information can be obtained from The FCC's Public Access Link (PAL) and the Office of Engineering and Technology (OET) Fee Filing Guide. See *"FCC's computer bulletin board"* and *"Obtaining forms and fee filing guides"* under **Additional Information** on pages 31 and 32 of this bulletin.

TABLE OF CONTENTS

FEDERAL COMMUNICATIONS COMMISSION
Office of Engineering and Technology
Washington, DC 20554

**UNDERSTANDING THE FCC REGULATIONS
FOR LOW-POWER, NON-LICENSED TRANSMITTERS**

OET Bulletin 63
October, 1993
Edited and reprinted Feb. 1996

Introduction

Low-power, non-licensed transmitters are used virtually everywhere. Cordless phones, baby monitors, garage door openers, wireless home security systems, keyless automobile entry systems and hundreds of other types of common electronic equipment rely on such transmitters to function. At any time of day, most people are within a few meters of consumer products that use low-power, non-licensed transmitters.

Non-licensed transmitters operate on a variety of frequencies. They must share these frequencies with licensed transmitters and are prohibited from causing interference to licensed transmitters.

The Federal Communications Commission (FCC) has rules to limit the potential for harmful interference to licensed transmitters by low-power, non-licensed transmitters. In its regulations, the FCC takes into account that different types of products that incorporate low-power transmitters have different potentials for causing harmful interference. As a result, the FCC's regulations are most restrictive on products that are most likely to cause harmful interference, and less restrictive on those that are least likely to cause interference.

This bulletin is intended to provide a general understanding of the FCC's regulations and policies applying to products using low-power transmitters. It reflects the current text and interpretations of the FCC's regulations. More detailed information is contained in the regulations themselves, which can be found in Part 15 of Title 47 of the Code of Federal Regulations. This bulletin does not replace or supersede those regulations.

Manufacturers and parties selling low-power, non-licensed transmitters, or products containing low-power, non-licensed transmitters, are strongly encouraged to review the FCC's regulations closely. Recognizing that new uses of low-power transmitters often generate questions that are not directly addressed in the regulations, we welcome inquiries or requests for specific interpretations. Occasionally, the FCC proposes changes to its regulations, generally to address industry concerns and/or as new uses of low-power transmission equipment appear. See the section titled **Additional Information** for information on obtaining the FCC regulations, requesting interpretations, and finding out about proposed rule changes.

Low-Power, Non-Licensed Transmitters

Throughout this bulletin the terms "low-power transmitter," "low-power, non-licensed transmitter," and "Part 15 transmitter" all refer to the same thing: a low-power, non-licensed transmitter that complies with the regulations in Part 15 of the FCC rules. Part 15 transmitters use very little power, most of them less than a milliwatt. They are "non-licensed" because their operators are not required to obtain a license from the FCC to use them.

Section 15.1

Although an operator does not have to obtain a license to use a Part 15 transmitter, the transmitter itself is required to have an FCC authorization before it can be legally marketed in the United States. This authorization requirement helps ensure that Part 15 transmitters comply with the Commission's technical standards and, thus, are capable of being operated with little potential for causing interference to authorized radio communications.

Section 15.201
Section 2.803

If a Part 15 transmitter does cause interference to authorized radio communications, even if the transmitter complies with all of the technical standards and equipment authorization requirements in the FCC rules, then its operator will be required to cease operation, at least until the interference problem is corrected.

Section 15.5

Part 15 transmitters receive no regulatory protection from interference.

Antenna Requirement

Changing the antenna on a transmitter can significantly increase, or decrease, the strength of the signal that is ultimately transmitted. Except for cable locating equipment, the standards in Part 15 are not based solely on output power but also take into account the antenna characteristics. Thus, a low power transmitter that complies with the technical standards in Part 15 with a particular antenna attached can exceed the Part 15 standards if a different antenna is attached. Should this happen it could pose a serious interference problem to authorized radio communications such as emergency, broadcast and air-traffic control communications.

In order to prevent such interference problems, each Part 15 transmitter must be designed to ensure that no type of antenna can be used with it other than the one used to demonstrate compliance with the technical standards. This means that Part 15 transmitters must have permanently attached antennas, or detachable antennas with unique connectors. A "unique connector" is one that is not of a standard type found in electronic supply stores.

Section 15.203

It is recognized that suppliers of Part 15 transmitters often want their customers to be able to replace an antenna if it should break. With this in mind, Part 15 allows transmitters to be designed so that the user can replace a broken antenna. When this is done, the replacement antenna must be electrically identical to the antenna that was used to obtain FCC authorization for the transmitter. The replacement antenna also must include the unique connector described above to ensure it is used with the proper transmitter.

Home-Built Transmitters that are Not for Sale

Hobbyists, inventors and other parties that design and build Part 15 transmitters with no intention of ever marketing them may construct and operate up to five such transmitters for their own personal use without having to obtain FCC equipment authorization. If possible, these transmitters should be tested for compliance with the Commission's rules. If such testing is not practicable, their designers and builders are required to employ good engineering practices in order to ensure compliance with the Part 15 standards.

Section 15.23

Home-built transmitters, like all Part 15 transmitters, are not allowed to cause interference to licensed radio communications and must accept any interference that they receive. If a home-built Part 15 transmitter does cause interference to licensed radio communications, the Commission will require its operator to cease operation until the interference problem is corrected. Furthermore, if the Commission determines that the operator of such a transmitter has not attempted to ensure compliance with the Part 15 technical standards by employing good engineering practices then that operator may be fined up to $10,000 for each violation and $75,000 for a repeat or continuing violation.

Section 15.5
47 U.S.C. 503

Operating a prototype of a product that is ultimately intended for market is not considered "personal use." Thus, a party that designs and builds a transmitter with plans to mass produce and market a future version of it must obtain an experimental license from the FCC in order to operate the transmitter for any purpose other than testing for compliance with the Part 15 technical standards. Information on experimental licenses may be obtained from the contact point listed in the **Additional Information** section of this bulletin. FCC authorization is not required in order to test a transmitter for compliance with the Part 15 technical standards.

Section 15.7
47 CFR Part 5

Equipment Authorization

A Part 15 transmitter must be tested and authorized before it may be marketed. There are two ways to obtain authorization: certification and verification.

Section 15.201
Section 2.803
47 U.S.C. 302(b)

Certification

The *certification* procedure requires that tests be performed to measure the levels of radio frequency energy that are radiated by the device into the open air or conducted by the device onto the power lines. A description of the measurement facilities of the laboratory where these tests are performed must be on file with the Commission's laboratory or must accompany the certification application. After these tests have been performed, a report must be produced showing the test procedure, the test results, and some additional information about the device including design drawings. The specific information that must be included in a certification report is detailed in Part 2 of the FCC Rules.

Section 2.948
Section 2.1033

Section 2.938
Section 2.1033

Certified transmitters also are required to have two labels attached: an FCC ID label and a compliance label. The FCC ID label identifies the FCC equipment authorization file that is associated with the transmitter, and serves as an indication to consumers that the transmitter has been authorized by the FCC. The compliance label indicates to consumers that the transmitter was authorized under Part 15 of the FCC rules and that it may not cause, nor is it protected from, harmful interference.

The FCC ID. The FCC ID must be permanently marked (etched, engraved, indelibly printed, etc.) either directly on the transmitter, or on a tag that is permanently affixed (riveted, welded, glued, etc.) to it. The FCC ID label must be readily visible to the purchaser at the time of purchase.

Section 2.925

The FCC ID is a string of 4 to 17 characters. It may contain any combination of capital letters, numbers, or the dash/hyphen character. Characters 4 through 17 may be designated, as desired, by the applicant. The first three characters, however, are the "grantee code," a code assigned by the FCC to each particular applicant (grantee). Any application filed with the FCC must have an FCC ID that begins with an assigned grantee code.

Section 2.925
Section 2.926

The Grantee Code. To obtain a code, new applicants must send in a letter stating the applicant's name and address and requesting a grantee code. This letter must be accompanied by a completed "Fee Advice Form" (FCC Form 159), and a $45 processing fee. See *Obtaining...filing packets* on page 31.

Section 1.1103

The Compliance Label. The applicant for a grant of certification is responsible for having the compliance label produced and for having it affixed to each device that is marketed or imported. The wording for the compliance label is in Part 15, and may be included on the same label as the FCC ID, if desired.

Section 15.19

The compliance label and FCC ID label may not be attached to any devices until a grant of certification has been obtained for the devices.

Section 2.926

Once the report demonstrating compliance with the technical standards has been completed, and the compliance label and FCC ID label have been designed, the party wishing to get the transmitter certified (it can be anyone) must file a copy of the report, an "Application for Equipment Authorization" (FCC Form 731) and an $845 application fee, with the FCC. See *Obtaining...filing packets* on page 31.

Section 2.911
Section 2.1033
Section 1.1103

After the application is submitted, the FCC's lab will review the report and may or may not request a sample of the transmitter to test. If the application is complete and accurate, and any tests performed by the FCC's lab confirm that the transmitter is compliant, the FCC will then issue a grant of certification for the transmitter. Marketing of the transmitter may begin after the applicant has received a copy of this grant.

Section 2.943
Section 2.803

Typically, 90% of the applications for certification that the FCC receives are processed within 30 calendar days. This time frame may increase due to incomplete applications and pre-grant sampling, if determined to be necessary.

Section 2.943

Verification

The *verification* procedure requires that tests be performed on the transmitter to be authorized using a laboratory that has calibrated its test site or, if the transmitter is incapable of being tested at a laboratory, at the installation site. These tests measure the levels of radio frequency energy that are radiated by the transmitter into the open air or conducted by the transmitter onto the power lines. After these tests are performed, a report must be produced showing the test procedure, the test results, and some additional information about the transmitter including design drawings. The specific information that must be included in a verification report is detailed in Part 2 of the FCC Rules.

Sections 2.951 through 2.957

Once the report is completed, the manufacturer (or importer for an imported device) is required to keep a copy of it on file as evidence that the transmitter meets the technical standards in Part 15. The manufacturer (importer) must be able to produce this report on short notice should the FCC ever request it.

Section 2.955 Section 2.956

The Compliance Label. The manufacturer (or importer) is responsible for having the compliance label produced, and for having it affixed to each transmitter that is marketed or imported. The wording for the compliance label is included in Part 15. Verified transmitters must be uniquely identified with a brand name and/or model number that cannot be confused with other, electrically different transmitters on the market. However, they may not be labelled with an FCC ID or in a manner that could be confused with an FCC ID.

Section 15.19 Section 2.954

Once the report showing compliance is in the manufacturer's (or importer's) files and the compliance label has been attached to the transmitter, marketing of the transmitter may begin. *There is no filing with the FCC required for verified equipment.*

Section 2.805

Any equipment that connects to the public switched telephone network, such as a cordless telephone, is also subject to regulations in Part 68 of the FCC Rules and must be registered by the FCC prior to marketing. The rules in Part 68 are designed to protect against harm to the telephone network.

Section 68.102

Authorization Procedures for Part 15 Transmitters

Low Power Transmitter	Authorization Procedure
AM-band transmission systems on the campuses of educational institutions	Verification
Cable locating equipment at or below 490 kHz	Verification
Carrier current systems	Verification
Devices, such as a perimeter protection systems, that must be measured at the installation site	Verification of first three installations with resulting data immediately used to obtain certification
Leaky coaxial cable systems	If designed for operation exclusively in the AM broadcast band: verification; otherwise: certification
Tunnel radio systems	Verification
All other Part 15 transmitters	Certification

The Verification Procedure **The Certification Procedure**

| TEST TRANSMITTER FOR RADIO FREQUENCY EMISSIONS (LAB FEES AND SPEED OF SERVICE VARY WIDELY - CONTACT SOME LABS IN YOUR AREA TO ESTIMATE SPEED AND COST OF SERVICE) |

| MAIL LETTER REQUESTING GRANTEE CODE, FCC FORM 159, AND $45 FILING FEE TO FCC'S MELLON BANK SERVICE CENTER IN PITTSBURGH, PA ONLY IF YOU'RE A NEW APPLICANT (7-10 DAY RESPONSE TIME)

TEST TRANSMITTER FOR RADIO FREQUENCY EMISSIONS (LAB FEES AND SPEED OF SERVICE VARY WIDELY - CONTACT SOME LABS IN YOUR AREA TO ESTIMATE SPEED AND COST OF SERVICE) |

Certification:
Sections 2.1031
through 2.1045

Verification:
Sections 2.951
through 2.957

ONCE TESTS INDICATE THAT TRANSMITTER COMPLIES WITH FCC STANDARDS, DESIGN COMPLIANCE LABEL AND AFFIX IT TO ALL DEVICES TO BE MARKETED

PRODUCE REPORT SHOWING TEST RESULTS

ONCE TESTS INDICATE THAT TRANSMITTER COMPLIES WITH FCC TECHNICAL STANDARDS, ASSIGN FCC ID TO TRANSMITTER AND DESIGN COMPLIANCE LABEL

MAINTAIN COPY OF TEST REPORT AND EQUIPMENT DESCRIPTION IN FILES OF MANUFACTURER (IMPORTER IF THE EQUIPMENT IS IMPORTED)

FILE FCC FORM 731, $845 FILING FEE, EMISSIONS TEST REPORT, AND OTHER INFORMATION REQUIRED BY THE RULES WITH FCC'S MELLON BANK SERVICE CENTER IN PITTSBURGH, PA (≈30 DAY RESPONSE TIME)

TRANSMITTER IS NOW VERIFIED AND MARKETING MAY BEGIN (NO FILING WITH THE FCC IS REQUIRED FOR VERIFICATION)

RECEIVE GRANT OF CERTIFICATION (OR DENIAL) IN MAIL FROM FCC

IF A GRANT IS RECEIVED, THE TRANSMITTER IS NOW CERTIFIED AND MARKETING MAY BEGIN

Technical Standards

Conducted emission limits

Part 15 transmitters that obtain power from the electrical power lines are subject to conducted emission standards that limit the amount of radio frequency energy they can conduct back onto these lines in the band 450 kHz - 30 MHz. This limit is 250 microvolts.

Section 15.207

An exception to the conducted emission requirements is made for carrier current systems. These systems are not subject to any conducted emission limits unless they produce emissions (fundamental or harmonic) in the 535 kHz - 1,705 kHz band and are not intended to be received by standard AM broadcast receivers, in which case they are subject to a 1,000 microvolt limit.

Although carrier current systems are, for the most part, not subject to conducted emission limits, they are still subject to radiated emission limits.

Radiated emission limits

Section 15.209 contains general radiated emission (signal strength) limits that apply to all Part 15 transmitters using frequencies at 9 kHz and above. There are also a number of *restricted bands* in which low power, non-licensed transmitters are not allowed to operate because of potential interference to sensitive radio communications such as aircraft radionavigation, radio astronomy and search and rescue operations. If a particular transmitter can comply with the general radiated limits, and at the same time avoid operating in one of the restricted bands, then it can use any type of modulation (AM, FM, PCM, etc.) for any purpose.

Section 15.209
Section 15.205

With the exception of intermittent and periodic transmissions, and biomedical telemetry devices, Part 15 transmitters are *not* permitted to operate in the TV broadcast bands.

Special provisions have been made in the Part 15 rules for certain types of transmitters that require a stronger signal strength on certain frequencies than the general radiated emission limits provide. For example, such provisions have been made for cordless telephones, auditory assistance devices and field disturbance sensors, among other things.

The following table illustrates where, in the radio frequency spectrum, the Part 15 restricted bands lie. The table after that illustrates what type of Part 15 operation is permitted for every frequency above 9 kHz, the emission limit for that type of operation, and the type of detector ("Det") used to measure emissions (average with a peak limit, "A," or quasi-peak, "Q"). When a transmitter power limit is specified instead of an emission limit, no emission detector is specified.

Section 15.209
Section 15.205
Sections 15.215
through 15.251
Section 15.35

7

The Part 15 Restricted Bands - Spurious Emissions Only

Section 15.205

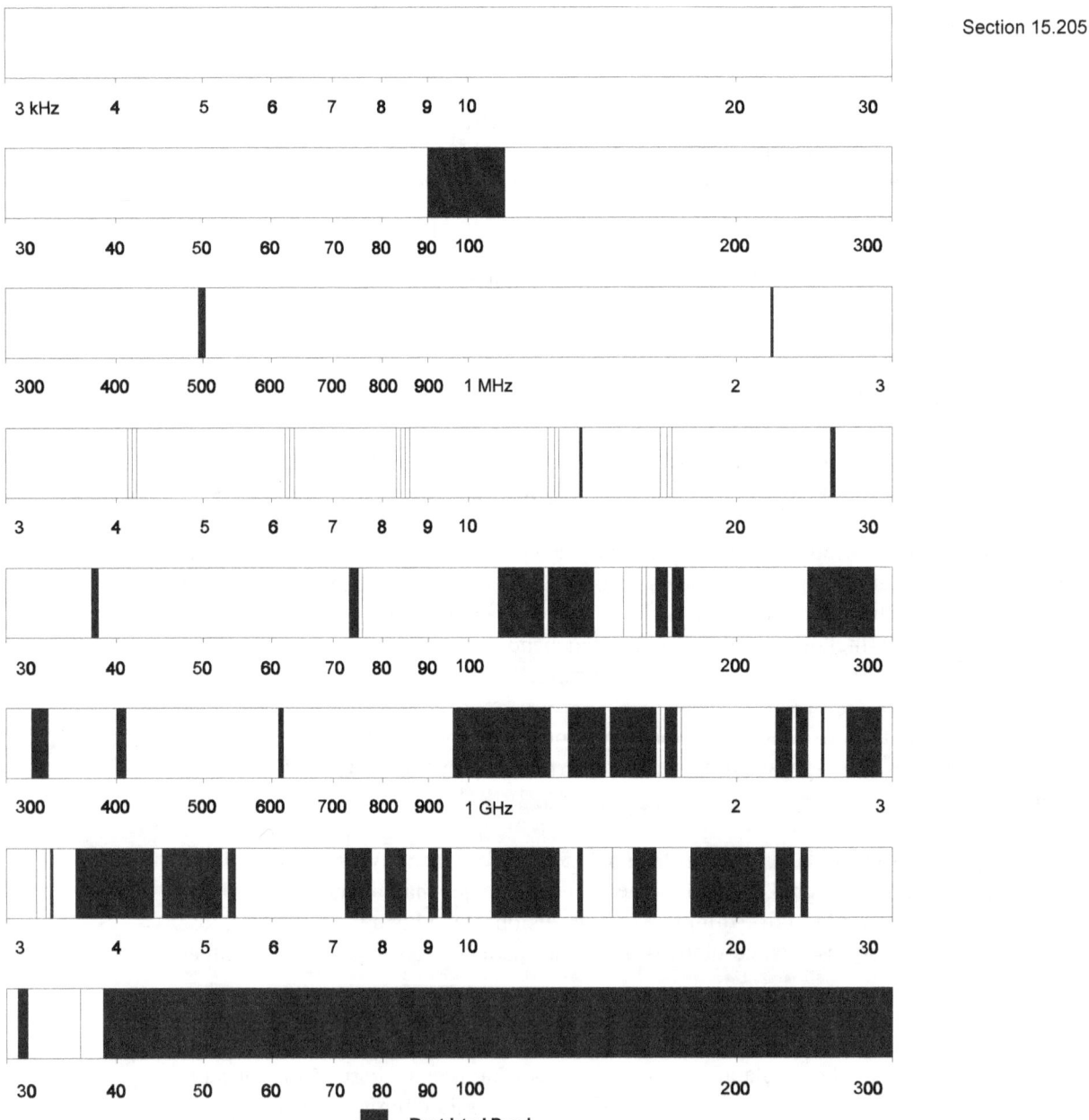

Restricted Band

8

Part 15 low-power transmitter frequency table

Frequency Band	Type of Use	Emission Limit	Det	47 CFR
9-45 kHz	Cable locating equipment	10 Watts peak output power		15.213
	Any	2400/f(kHz) μV/m @ 300 m	A	15.209
45-90 kHz	Cable locating equipment	1 Watt peak output power		15.213
	Any	2400/f(kHz) μV/m @ 300 m	A	15.209
90-101.4 kHz	Cable locating equipment	1 Watt peak output power		15.213
101.4 kHz	Cable locating equipment	1 Watt peak output power		15.213
	Telephone company electronic marker detectors	23.7 μV/m @ 300 m	A	15.205
101.4-110 kHz	Cable locating equipment	1 Watt peak output power		15.213
110-160 kHz	Cable locating equipment	1 Watt peak output power		15.213
	Any	2400/f(kHz) μV/m @ 300 m	A	15.209
160-190 kHz	Cable locating equipment	1 Watt peak output power		15.213
	Any	1 Watt input to final RF stage		15.217
	Any	2400/f(kHz) μV/m @ 300 m	A	15.209
190-490 kHz	Cable locating equipment	1 Watt peak output power		15.213
	Any	2400/f(kHz) μV/m @ 300 m	A	15.209
490-495 kHz (before 2/1/99)	SPURIOUS EMISSIONS ONLY	24000/f(kHz) μV/m @ 30 m	Q	15.205
490-495 kHz (cont.) (on or after 2/1/99)	Any	24000/f(kHz) μV/m @ 30 m	Q	15.209
495-505 kHz	SPURIOUS EMISSIONS ONLY	24000/f(kHz) μV/m @ 30 m	Q	15.205
505-510 kHz (before 2/1/99)	SPURIOUS EMISSIONS ONLY	24000/f(kHz) μV/m @ 30 m	Q	15.205
(on or after 2/1/99)	Any	24000/f(kHz) μV/m @ 30 m	Q	15.209

Frequency	Type	Field strength / Power	Detector	Rule
510-525 kHz	Any	100 mW input to final RF stage		15.219
	Any	24000/f(kHz) µV/m @ 30 m	Q	15.209
525-1705 kHz	Any	100 mW input to final RF stage		15.219
	Transmitters on grounds of educational institutions	24000/f(kHz) µV/m @ 30 m outside of campus boundary	Q	15.221
	Carrier current & leaky coax systems	15 µV/m @ 47,715/f(kHz) m from cable	Q	15.221
	Any	24000/f(kHz) µV/m @ 30 m	Q	15.209
1.705-2.1735 MHz	Any, when 6 dB bandwidth ≥ 10% of center frequency	100 µV/m @ 30 m	A	15.223
	Any, when 6 dB bandwidth < 10% of center frequency	15 µV/m @ 30 m or bandwidth in (kHz) / f(MHz)	A	15.223
	Any	30 µV/m @ 30 m	Q	15.209
2.1735-2.1905 MHz	Swept frequency field disturbance sensors	30 µV/m @ 30 m	Q	15.205
2.1905-4.125 MHz	Any, when 6 dB bandwidth ≥ 10% of center frequency	100 µV/m @ 30 m	A	15.223
	Any, when 6 dB bandwidth < 10% of center frequency	15 µV/m @ 30 m or bandwidth in (kHz) / f(MHz)	A	15.223
	Any	30 µV/m @ 30 m	Q	15.209
4.125-4.128 MHz	Swept frequency field disturbance sensors	30 µV/m @ 30 m	Q	15.205
4.128-4.17725 MHz	Any, when 6 dB bandwidth ≥ 10% of center frequency	100 µV/m @ 30 m	A	15.223
	Any, when 6 dB bandwidth < 10% of center frequency	15 µV/m @ 30 m or bandwidth in (kHz) / f(MHz)	A	15.223
	Any	30 µV/m @ 30 m	Q	15.209
4.17725-4.17775 MHz	Swept frequency field disturbance sensors	30 µV/m @ 30 m	Q	15.205
4.17775-4.20725 MHz	Any, when 6 dB bandwidth ≥ 10% of center frequency	100 µV/m @ 30 m	A	15.223
	Any, when 6 dB bandwidth < 10% of center frequency	15 µV/m @ 30 m or bandwidth in (kHz) / f(MHz)	A	15.223

	Any	30 μV/m @ 30 m	Q	15.209
4.20725-4.20775 MHz	Swept frequency field disturbance sensors	30 μV/m @ 30 m	Q	15.205
4.20775-6.215 MHz	Any, when 6 dB bandwidth ≥ 10% of center frequency	100 μV/m @ 30 m	A	15.223
	Any, when 6 dB bandwidth < 10% of center frequency	15 μV/m @ 30 m or bandwidth in (kHz) / f(MHz)	A	15.223
	Any	30 μV/m @ 30 m	Q	15.209
6.215-6.218 MHz	Swept frequency field disturbance sensors	30 μV/m @ 30 m	Q	15.205
6.218-6.26775 MHz	Any, when 6 dB bandwidth ≥ 10% of center frequency	100 μV/m @ 30 m	A	15.223
	Any, when 6 dB bandwidth < 10% of center frequency	15 μV/m @ 30 m or bandwidth in (kHz) / f(MHz)	A	15.223
	Any	30 μV/m @ 30 m	Q	15.209
6.26775-6.26825 MHz	Swept frequency field disturbance sensors	30 μV/m @ 30 m	Q	15.205
6.26825-6.31175 MHz	Any, when 6 dB bandwidth ≥ 10% of center frequency	100 μV/m @ 30 m	A	15.223
	Any, when 6 dB bandwidth < 10% of center frequency	15 μV/m @ 30 m or bandwidth in (kHz) / f(MHz)	A	15.223
	Any	30 μV/m @ 30 m	Q	15.209
6.31175-6.31225 MHz	Swept frequency field disturbance sensors	30 μV/m @ 30 m	Q	15.205
6.31225-8.291 MHz	Any, when 6 dB bandwidth ≥ 10% of center frequency	100 μV/m @ 30 m	A	15.223
	Any, when 6 dB bandwidth < 10% of center frequency	15 μV/m @ 30 m or bandwidth in (kHz) / f(MHz)	A	15.223
	Any	30 μV/m @ 30 m	Q	15.209
8.291-8.294 MHz	Swept frequency field disturbance sensors	30 μV/m @ 30 m	Q	15.205
8.294-8.362 MHz	Any, when 6 dB bandwidth ≥ 10% of center frequency	100 μV/m @ 30 m	A	15.223
	Any, when 6 dB bandwidth < 10% of center frequency	15 μV/m @ 30 m or bandwidth in (kHz) / f(MHz)	A	15.223
	Any	30 μV/m @ 30 m	Q	15.209

8.362-8.366 MHz	Swept frequency field disturbance sensors	30 μV/m @ 30 m	Q	15.205
8.366-8.37625 MHz	Any, when 6 dB bandwidth ≥ 10% of center frequency	100 μV/m @ 30 m	A	15.223
	Any, when 6 dB bandwidth < 10% of center frequency	15 μV/m @ 30 m or bandwidth in (kHz) / f(MHz)	A	15.223
	Any	30 μV/m @ 30 m	Q	15.209
8.37625-8.38675 MHz	Swept frequency field disturbance sensors	30 μV/m @ 30 m	Q	15.205
8.38675-8.41425 MHz	Any, when 6 dB bandwidth ≥ 10% of center frequency	100 μV/m @ 30 m	A	15.223
8.38675-8.41425 MHz (cont.)	Any, when 6 dB bandwidth < 10% of center frequency	15 μV/m @ 30 m or bandwidth in (kHz) / f(MHz)	A	15.223
	Any	30 μV/m @ 30 m	Q	15.209
8.41425-8.41475 MHz	Swept frequency field disturbance sensors	30 μV/m @ 30 m	Q	15.205
8.41475-10 MHz	Any, when 6 dB bandwidth ≥ 10% of center frequency	100 μV/m @ 30 m	A	15.223
	Any, when 6 dB bandwidth < 10% of center frequency	15 μV/m @ 30 m or bandwidth in (kHz) / f(MHz)	A	15.223
	Any	30 μV/m @ 30 m	Q	15.209
10-12.29 MHz	Any	30 μV/m @ 30 m	Q	15.209
12.29-12.293 MHz	Swept frequency field disturbance sensors	30 μV/m @ 30 m	Q	15.205
12.293-12.51975 MHz	Any	30 μV/m @ 30 m	Q	15.209
12.51975-12.52025 MHz	Swept frequency field disturbance sensors	30 μV/m @ 30 m	Q	15.205
12.52025-12.57675 MHz	Any	30 μV/m @ 30 m	Q	15.209
12.57675-12.57725 MHz	Swept frequency field disturbance sensors	30 μV/m @ 30 m	Q	15.205
12.57725-13.36 MHz	Any	30 μV/m @ 30 m	Q	15.209
13.36-13.41 MHz	Swept frequency field disturbance sensors	30 μV/m @ 30 m	Q	15.205
13.41-13.553 MHz	Any	30 μV/m @ 30 m	Q	15.209

13.553-13.567 MHz	Any	10,000 μV/m @ 30 m	Q	15.225
	Any	30 μV/m @ 30 m	Q	15.209
13.567-16.42 MHz	Any	30 μV/m @ 30 m	Q	15.209
16.42-16.423 MHz	Swept frequency field disturbance sensors	30 μV/m @ 30 m	Q	15.205
16.423-16.69475 MHz	Any	30 μV/m @ 30 m	Q	15.209
16.69475-16.69525 MHz	Swept frequency field disturbance sensors	30 μV/m @ 30 m	Q	15.205
16.69525-16.80425 MHz	Any	30 μV/m @ 30 m	Q	15.209
16.80425-16.80475 MHz	Swept frequency field disturbance sensors	30 μV/m @ 30 m	Q	15.205
16.80475-25.5 MHz	Any	30 μV/m @ 30 m	Q	15.209
25.5-25.67 MHz	Swept frequency field disturbance sensors	30 μV/m @ 30 m	Q	15.205
25.67-26.96 MHz	Any	30 μV/m @ 30 m	Q	15.209
26.96-27.28 MHz	Any	10,000 μV/m @ 3 m	A	15.227
	Any	30 μV/m @ 30 m	Q	15.209
27.28-30 MHz	Any	30 μV/m @ 30 m	Q	15.209
30-37.5 MHz	Any	100 μV/m @ 3 m	Q	15.209
37.5-38.25 MHz	SPURIOUS EMISSIONS ONLY	100 μV/m @ 3 m	Q	15.205
38.25-40.66 MHz	Any	100 μV/m @ 3 m	Q	15.209
40.66-40.7 MHz	Intermittent Control Signals	2,250 μV/m @ 3 m	A or Q	15.231
	Periodic Transmissions	1,000 μV/m @ 3 m	A or Q	15.231
	Any	1,000 μV/m @ 3 m	Q	15.229
	Perimeter Protection Systems	500 μV/m @ 3 m	A	15.229
40.7-43.71 MHz	Any	100 μV/m @ 3 m	Q	15.209
43.71-44.49 MHz	Cordless Telephones	10,000 μV/m @ 3 m	A	15.233

	Any	100 µV/m @ 3 m	Q	15.209
44.49-46.6 MHz	Any	100 µV/m @ 3 m	Q	15.209
46.6-46.98 MHz	Cordless Telephones	10,000 µV/m @ 3 m	A	15.233
	Any	100 µV/m @ 3 m	Q	15.209
46.98-48.75 MHz	Any	100 µV/m @ 3 m	Q	15.209
48.75-49.51 MHz	Cordless Telephones	10,000 µV/m @ 3 m	A	15.233
	Any	100 µV/m @ 3 m	Q	15.209
49.51-49.66 MHz	Any	100 µV/m @ 3 m	Q	15.209
49.66-49.82 MHz	Cordless Telephones	10,000 µV/m @ 3 m	A	15.233
	Any	100 µV/m @ 3 m	Q	15.209
49.82-49.9 MHz	Any	10,000 µV/m @ 3 m	A	15.235
	Cordless Telephones	10,000 µV/m @ 3 m	A	15.233
49.9-50 MHz	Cordless Telephones	10,000 µV/m @ 3 m	A	15.233
	Any	100 µV/m @ 3 m	Q	15.209
50-54 MHz	Any	100 µV/m @ 3 m	Q	15.209
54-70 MHz	Non-Residential Perimeter Protection Systems	100 µV/m @ 3 m	Q	15.209
70-72 MHz	Intermittent Control Signals	1,250 µV/m @ 3 m	A or Q	15.231
	Periodic Transmissions	500 µV/m @ 3 m	A or Q	15.231
	Non-Residential Perimeter Protection Systems	100 µV/m @ 3 m	Q	15.209
72-73 MHz	Auditory Assistance Devices	80,000 µV/m @ 3 m	A	15.237
	Intermittent Control Signals	1,250 µV/m @ 3 m	A or Q	15.231
	Periodic Transmissions	500 µV/m @ 3 m	A or Q	15.231
	Any	100 µV/m @ 3 m	Q	15.209

14

Frequency	Device Type	Field Strength	A/Q	Rule
73-74.6 MHz	SPURIOUS EMISSIONS ONLY	100 µV/m @ 3 m	Q	15.205
74.6-74.8 MHz	Auditory Assistance Devices	80,000 µV/m @ 3 m	A	15.237
	Intermittent Control Signals	1,250 µV/m @ 3 m	A or Q	15.231
	Periodic Transmissions	500 µV/m @ 3 m	A or Q	15.231
	Any	100 µV/m @ 3 m	Q	15.209
74.8-75.2 MHz	SPURIOUS EMISSIONS ONLY	100 µV/m @ 3 m	Q	15.205
75.2-76 MHz	Auditory Assistance Devices	80,000 µV/m @ 3 m	A	15.237
	Intermittent Control Signals	1,250 µV/m @ 3 m	A or Q	15.231
	Periodic Transmissions	500 µV/m @ 3 m	A or Q	15.231
	Any	100 µV/m @ 3 m	Q	15.209
76-88 MHz	Intermittent Control Signals	1,250 µV/m @ 3 m	A or Q	15.231
	Periodic Transmissions	500 µV/m @ 3 m	A or Q	15.231
	Non-Residential Perimeter Protection Systems	100 µV/m @ 3 m	Q	15.209
88-108 MHz	Intermittent Control Signals	1,250 µV/m @ 3 m	A or Q	15.231
	Periodic Transmissions	500 µV/m @ 3 m	A or Q	15.231
	Any (≤ 200 kHz bandwidth)	250 µV/m @ 3 m	A	15.239
	Any	150 µV/m @ 3 m	Q	15.209
108-121.94 MHz	SPURIOUS EMISSIONS ONLY	150 µV/m @ 3 m	Q	15.205
121.94-123 MHz	Intermittent Control Signals	1,250 µV/m @ 3 m	A or Q	15.231
	Periodic Transmissions	500 µV/m @ 3 m	A or Q	15.231
121.94-123 MHz (cont.)	Any	150 µV/m @ 3 m	Q	15.209
123-138 MHz	SPURIOUS EMISSIONS ONLY	150 µV/m @ 3 m	Q	15.205

138-149.9 MHz	Intermittent Control Signals	(625/11) x f(MHz) - (67500/11) µV/m @ 3 m	A or Q	15.231
	Periodic Transmissions	(250/11) x f(MHz) - (27000/11) µV/m @ 3 m	A or Q	15.231
	Any	150 µV/m @ 3 m	Q	15.209
149.9-150.05 MHz	SPURIOUS EMISSIONS ONLY	150 µV/m @ 3 m	Q	15.205
150.05-156.52475 MHz	Intermittent Control Signals	(625/11) x f(MHz) - (67500/11) µV/m @ 3 m	A or Q	15.231
	Periodic Transmissions	(250/11) x f(MHz) - (27000/11) µV/m @ 3 m	A or Q	15.231
	Any	150 µV/m @ 3 m	Q	15.209
156.52475-156.52525 MHz	SPURIOUS EMISSIONS ONLY	150 µV/m @ 3 m	Q	15.205
156.52525-156.7 MHz	Intermittent Control Signals	(625/11) x f(MHz) - (67500/11) µV/m @ 3 m	A or Q	15.231
	Periodic Transmissions	(250/11) x f(MHz) - (27000/11) µV/m @ 3 m	A or Q	15.231
	Any	150 µV/m @ 3 m	Q	15.209
156.7-156.9 MHz	SPURIOUS EMISSIONS ONLY	150 µV/m @ 3 m	Q	15.205
156.9-162.0125 MHz	Intermittent Control Signals	(625/11) x f(MHz) - (67500/11) µV/m @ 3 m	A or Q	15.231
	Periodic Transmissions	(250/11) x f(MHz) - (27000/11) µV/m @ 3 m	A or Q	15.231
156.9-162.0125 MHz (cont.)	Any	150 µV/m @ 3 m	Q	15.209
162.0125-167.17 MHz	SPURIOUS EMISSIONS ONLY	150 µV/m @ 3 m	Q	15.205
167.17-167.72 MHz	Intermittent Control Signals	(625/11) x f(MHz) - (67500/11) µV/m @ 3 m	A or Q	15.231
	Periodic Transmissions	(250/11) x f(MHz) - (27000/11) µV/m @ 3 m	A or Q	15.231
	Any	150 µV/m @ 3 m	Q	15.209

16

167.72-173.2 MHz	SPURIOUS EMISSIONS ONLY	150 µV/m @ 3 m	Q	15.205
173.2-174 MHz	Intermittent Control Signals	(625/11) x f(MHz) - (67500/11) µV/m @ 3 m	A or Q	15.231
	Periodic Transmissions	(250/11) x f(MHz) - (27000/11) µV/m @ 3 m	A or Q	15.231
	Any	150 µV/m @ 3 m	Q	15.209
174-216 MHz	Intermittent Control Signals	3,750 µV/m @ 3 m	A or Q	15.231
	Periodic Transmissions	1,500 µV/m @ 3 m	A or Q	15.231
	Biomedical Telemetry Devices	1,500 µV/m @ 3 m	A	15.241
216-240 MHz	Intermittent Control Signals	3,750 µV/m @ 3 m	A or Q	15.231
	Periodic Transmissions	1,500 µV/m @ 3 m	A or Q	15.231
	Any	200 µV/m @ 3 m	Q	15.209
240-285 MHz	SPURIOUS EMISSIONS ONLY	200 µV/m @ 3 m	Q	15.205
285-322 MHz 285-322 MHz (cont.)	Intermittent Control Signals	(125/3) x f(MHz) (21250/3) µV/m @ 3 m	A or Q	15.231
	Periodic Transmissions	(50/3) x f(MHz) - (8500/3) µV/m @ 3 m	A or Q	15.231
	Any	200 µV/m @ 3 m	Q	15.209
322-335.4 MHz	SPURIOUS EMISSIONS ONLY	200 µV/m @ 3 m	Q	15.205
335.4-399.9 MHz	Intermittent Control Signals	(125/3) x f(MHz) - (21250/3) µV/m @ 3 m	A or Q	15.231
	Periodic Transmissions	(50/3) x f(MHz) - (8500/3) µV/m @ 3 m	A or Q	15.231
	Any	200 µV/m @ 3 m	Q	15.209
399.9-410 MHz	SPURIOUS EMISSIONS ONLY	200 µV/m @ 3 m	Q	15.205
410-470 MHz	Intermittent Control Signals	(125/3) x f(MHz) - (21250/3) µV/m @ 3 m	A or Q	15.231

	Periodic Transmissions	(50/3) x f(MHz) - (8500/3) µV/m @ 3 m	A or Q	15.231
	Any	200 µV/m @ 3 m	Q	15.209
470-512 MHz	Intermittent Control Signals	12,500 µV/m @ 3 m	A or Q	15.231
	Periodic Transmissions	5,000 µV/m @ 3 m	A or Q	15.231
512-566 MHz	Intermittent Control Signals	12,500 µV/m @ 3 m	A or Q	15.231
	Periodic Transmissions	5,000 µV/m @ 3 m	A or Q	15.231
	Biomedical Telemetry Devices for Hospitals	200 µV/m @ 3 m	Q	15.209
566-608 MHz	Intermittent Control Signals	12,500 µV/m @ 3 m	A or Q	15.231
	Periodic Transmissions	5,000 µV/m @ 3 m	A or Q	15.231
608-614 MHz	SPURIOUS EMISSIONS ONLY	200 µV/m @ 3 m	Q	15.205
614-806 MHz	Intermittent Control Signals	12,500 µV/m @ 3 m	A or Q	15.231
	Periodic Transmissions	5,000 µV/m @ 3 m	A or Q	15.231
806-890 MHz	Intermittent Control Signals	12,500 µV/m @ 3 m	A or Q	15.231
	Periodic Transmissions	5,000 µV/m @ 3 m	A or Q	15.231
	Any	200 µV/m @ 3 m	Q	15.209
890-902 MHz	Intermittent Control Signals	12,500 µV/m @ 3 m	A or Q	15.231
	Periodic Transmissions	5,000 µV/m @ 3 m	A or Q	15.231
	Signals Used to Measure the Characteristics of a Material	500 µV/m @ 30 m	A	15.243
	Any	200 µV/m @ 3 m	Q	15.209
902-928 MHz	Spread Spectrum Transmitters	1 Watt Output Power		15.247
	Field Disturbance Sensors	500,000 µV/m @ 3 m	A	15.245
	Any	50,000 µV/m @ 3 m	Q	15.249

	Signals Used to Measure the Characteristics of a Material	500 μV/m @ 30 m	A	15.243
	Intermittent Control Signals	12,500 μV/m @ 3 m	A or Q	15.231
	Periodic Transmissions	5,000 μV/m @ 3 m	A or Q	15.231
928-940 MHz	Intermittent Control Signals	12,500 μV/m @ 3 m	A or Q	15.231
	Periodic Transmissions	5,000 μV/m @ 3 m	A or Q	15.231
	Signals Used to Measure the Characteristics of a Material	500 μV/m @ 30 m	A	15.243
928-940 MHz (cont.)	Any	200 μV/m @ 3 m	Q	15.209
940-960 MHz	Intermittent Control Signals	12,500 μV/m @ 3 m	A or Q	15.231
	Periodic Transmissions	5,000 μV/m @ 3 m	A or Q	15.231
	Any	200 μV/m @ 3 m	Q	15.209
960-1000 MHz	SPURIOUS EMISSIONS ONLY	500 μV/m @ 3 m	Q	15.205
1-1.24 GHz	SPURIOUS EMISSIONS ONLY	500 μV/m @ 3 m	A	15.205
1.24-1.3 GHz	Intermittent Control Signals	12,500 μV/m @ 3 m	A	15.231
	Periodic Transmissions	5,000 μV/m @ 3 m	A	15.231
	Any	500 μV/m @ 3 m	A	15.209
1.3-1.427 GHz	SPURIOUS EMISSIONS ONLY	500 μV/m @ 3 m	A	15.205
1.427-1.435 GHz	Intermittent Control Signals	12,500 μV/m @ 3 m	A	15.231
	Periodic Transmissions	5,000 μV/m @ 3 m	A	15.231
	Any	500 μV/m @ 3 m	A	15.209
1.435-1.6265 GHz	SPURIOUS EMISSIONS ONLY	500 μV/m @ 3 m	A	15.205
1.6265-1.6455 GHz	Intermittent Control Signals	12,500 μV/m @ 3 m	A	15.231
	Periodic Transmissions	5,000 μV/m @ 3 m	A	15.231
	Any	500 μV/m @ 3 m	A	15.209

1.6455-1.6465 GHz	SPURIOUS EMISSIONS ONLY	500 µV/m @ 3 m	A	15.205
1.6465-1.66 GHz	Intermittent Control Signals	12,500 µV/m @ 3 m	A	15.231
1.6465-1.66 GHz (cont.)	Periodic Transmissions	5,000 µV/m @ 3 m	A	15.231
	Any	500 µV/m @ 3 m	A	15.209
1.66-1.71 GHz	SPURIOUS EMISSIONS ONLY	500 µV/m @ 3 m	A	15.205
1.71-1.7188 GHz	Intermittent Control Signals	12,500 µV/m @ 3 m	A	15.231
	Periodic Transmissions	5,000 µV/m @ 3 m	A	15.231
	Any	500 µV/m @ 3 m	A	15.209
1.7188-1.7222 GHz	SPURIOUS EMISSIONS ONLY	500 µV/m @ 3 m	A	15.205
1.7222-2.2 GHz	Intermittent Control Signals	12,500 µV/m @ 3 m	A	15.231
	Periodic Transmissions	5,000 µV/m @ 3 m	A	15.231
	Any	500 µV/m @ 3 m	A	15.209
2.2-2.3 GHz	SPURIOUS EMISSIONS ONLY	500 µV/m @ 3 m	A	15.205
2.3-2.31 GHz	Intermittent Control Signals	12,500 µV/m @ 3 m	A	15.231
	Periodic Transmissions	5,000 µV/m @ 3 m	A	15.231
	Any	500 µV/m @ 3 m	A	15.209
2.31-2.39 GHz	SPURIOUS EMISSIONS ONLY	500 µV/m @ 3 m	A	15.205
2.39-2.4 GHz	Intermittent Control Signals	12,500 µV/m @ 3 m	A	15.231
	Periodic Transmissions	5,000 µV/m @ 3 m	A	15.231
	Any	500 µV/m @ 3 m	A	15.209
2.4-2.435 GHz	Spread Spectrum Transmitters	1 Watt Output Power		15.247
2.4-2.435 GHz (cont.)	Any	50,000 µV/m @ 3 m	A	15.249
2.435-2.465 GHz	Spread Spectrum Transmitters	1 Watt Output Power		15.247

	Field Disturbance Sensors	500,000 µV/m @ 3 m	A	15.245
	Any	50,000 µV/m @ 3 m	A	15.249
2.465-2.4835 GHz	Spread Spectrum Transmitters	1 Watt Output Power		15.247
	Any	50,000 µV/m @ 3 m	A	15.249
2.4835-2.5 GHz	SPURIOUS EMISSIONS ONLY	500 µV/m @ 3 m	A	15.205
2.5-2.655 GHz	Intermittent Control Signals	12,500 µV/m @ 3 m	A	15.231
	Periodic Transmissions	5,000 µV/m @ 3 m	A	15.231
	Any	500 µV/m @ 3 m	A	15.209
2.655-2.9 GHz	SPURIOUS EMISSIONS ONLY	500 µV/m @ 3 m	A	15.205
2.9-3.26 GHz	Intermittent Control Signals	12,500 µV/m @ 3 m	A	15.231
	Periodic Transmissions	5,000 µV/m @ 3 m	A	15.231
	Automatic Vehicle Identification Systems	3,000 µV/m per MHz of bandwidth @ 3 m	A	15.251
	Any	500 µV/m @ 3 m	A	15.209
3.26-3.267 GHz	SPURIOUS EMISSIONS ONLY	500 µV/m @ 3 m	A	15.205
3.267-3.332 GHz	Intermittent Control Signals	12,500 µV/m @ 3 m	A	15.231
	Periodic Transmissions	5,000 µV/m @ 3 m	A	15.231
	Automatic Vehicle Identification Systems	3,000 µV/m per MHz of bandwidth @ 3 m	A	15.251
3.267-3.332 GHz (cont.)	Any	500 µV/m @ 3 m	A	15.209
3.332-3.339 GHz	SPURIOUS EMISSIONS ONLY	500 µV/m @ 3 m	A	15.205
3.339-3.3458 GHz	Intermittent Control Signals	12,500 µV/m @ 3 m	A	15.231
	Periodic Transmissions	5,000 µV/m @ 3 m	A	15.231
	Automatic Vehicle Identification Systems	3,000 µV/m per MHz of bandwidth @ 3 m	A	15.251
	Any	500 µV/m @ 3 m	A	15.209

3.3458-3.358 GHz	SPURIOUS EMISSIONS ONLY	500 µV/m @ 3 m	A	15.205
3.358-3.6 GHz	Intermittent Control Signals	12,500 µV/m @ 3 m	A	15.231
	Periodic Transmissions	5,000 µV/m @ 3 m	A	15.231
	Automatic Vehicle Identification Systems	3,000 µV/m per MHz of bandwidth @ 3 m	A	15.251
	Any	500 µV/m @ 3 m	A	15.209
3.6-4.4 GHz	SPURIOUS EMISSIONS ONLY	500 µV/m @ 3 m	A	15.205
4.4-4.5 GHz	Intermittent Control Signals	12,500 µV/m @ 3 m	A	15.231
	Periodic Transmissions	5,000 µV/m @ 3 m	A	15.231
	Any	500 µV/m @ 3 m	A	15.209
4.5-5.25 GHz	SPURIOUS EMISSIONS ONLY	500 µV/m @ 3 m	A	15.205
5.25-5.35 GHz	Intermittent Control Signals	12,500 µV/m @ 3 m	A	15.231
	Periodic Transmissions	5,000 µV/m @ 3 m	A	15.231
	Any	500 µV/m @ 3 m	A	15.209
5.35-5.46 GHz	SPURIOUS EMISSIONS ONLY	500 µV/m @ 3 m	A	15.205
5.46-5.725 GHz	Intermittent Control Signals	12,500 µV/m @ 3 m	A	15.231
	Periodic Transmissions	5,000 µV/m @ 3 m	A	15.231
	Any	500 µV/m @ 3 m	A	15.209
5.725-5.785 GHz	Spread Spectrum Transmitters	1 Watt Output Power		15.247
	Any	50,000 µV/m @ 3 m	A	15.249
5.785-5.815 GHz	Spread Spectrum Transmitters	1 Watt Output Power		15.247
	Field Disturbance Sensors	500,000 µV/m @ 3 m	A	15.245
	Any	50,000 µV/m @ 3 m	A	15.249
5.815-5.85 GHz	Spread Spectrum Transmitters	1 Watt Output Power		15.247

	Any	50,000 µV/m @ 3 m	A	15.249
5.85-5.875 GHz	Any	50,000 µV/m @ 3 m	A	15.249
5.875-7.25 GHz	Intermittent Control Signals	12,500 µV/m @ 3 m	A	15.231
	Periodic Transmissions	5,000 µV/m @ 3 m	A	15.231
	Any	500 µV/m @ 3 m	A	15.209
7.25-7.75 GHz	SPURIOUS EMISSIONS ONLY	500 µV/m @ 3 m	A	15.205
7.75-8.025 GHz	Intermittent Control Signals	12,500 µV/m @ 3 m	A	15.231
	Periodic Transmissions	5,000 µV/m @ 3 m	A	15.231
	Any	500 µV/m @ 3 m	A	15.209
8.025-8.5 GHz	SPURIOUS EMISSIONS ONLY	500 µV/m @ 3 m	A	15.205
8.5-9 GHz	Intermittent Control Signals	12,500 µV/m @ 3 m	A	15.231
	Periodic Transmissions	5,000 µV/m @ 3 m	A	15.231
	Any	500 µV/m @ 3 m	A	15.209
9-9.2 GHz	SPURIOUS EMISSIONS ONLY	500 µV/m @ 3 m	A	15.205
9.2-9.3 GHz	Intermittent Control Signals	12,500 µV/m @ 3 m	A	15.231
	Periodic Transmissions	5,000 µV/m @ 3 m	A	15.231
	Any	500 µV/m @ 3 m	A	15.209
9.3-9.5 GHz	SPURIOUS EMISSIONS ONLY	500 µV/m @ 3 m	A	15.205
9.5-10.5 GHz	Intermittent Control Signals	12,500 µV/m @ 3 m	A	15.231
	Periodic Transmissions	5,000 µV/m @ 3 m	A	15.231
	Any	500 µV/m @ 3 m	A	15.209
10.5-10.55 GHz	Field Disturbance Sensors	2,500,000 µV/m @ 3 m	A	15.245
	Intermittent Control Signals	12,500 µV/m @ 3 m	A	15.231

	Periodic Transmissions	5,000 µV/m @ 3 m	A	15.231
	Any	500 µV/m @ 3 m	A	15.209
10.55-10.6 GHz	Intermittent Control Signals	12,500 µV/m @ 3 m	A	15.231
	Periodic Transmissions	5,000 µV/m @ 3 m	A	15.231
	Any	500 µV/m @ 3 m	A	15.209
10.6-12.7 GHz	SPURIOUS EMISSIONS ONLY	500 µV/m @ 3 m	A	15.205
12.7-13.25 GHz	Intermittent Control Signals	12,500 µV/m @ 3 m	A	15.231
	Periodic Transmissions	5,000 µV/m @ 3 m	A	15.231
	Any	500 µV/m @ 3 m	A	15.209
13.25-13.4 GHz	SPURIOUS EMISSIONS ONLY	500 µV/m @ 3 m	A	15.205
13.4-14.47 GHz	Intermittent Control Signals	12,500 µV/m @ 3 m	A	15.231
	Periodic Transmissions	5,000 µV/m @ 3 m	A	15.231
	Any	500 µV/m @ 3 m	A	15.209
14.47-14.5 GHz	SPURIOUS EMISSIONS ONLY	500 µV/m @ 3 m	A	15.205
14.5-15.35 GHz	Intermittent Control Signals	12,500 µV/m @ 3 m	A	15.231
	Periodic Transmissions	5,000 µV/m @ 3 m	A	15.231
	Any	500 µV/m @ 3 m	A	15.209
15.35-16.2 GHz	SPURIOUS EMISSIONS ONLY	500 µV/m @ 3 m	A	15.205
16.2-17.7 GHz	Intermittent Control Signals	12,500 µV/m @ 3 m	A	15.231
	Periodic Transmissions	5,000 µV/m @ 3 m	A	15.231
	Any	500 µV/m @ 3 m	A	15.209
17.7-21.4 GHz	SPURIOUS EMISSIONS ONLY	500 µV/m @ 3 m with higher emissions permitted according to Section 15.205(d)	A	15.205

21.4-22.01 GHz	Intermittent Control Signals	12,500 µV/m @ 3 m	A	15.231
21.4-22.01 GHz (cont.)	Periodic Transmissions	5,000 µV/m @ 3 m	A	15.231
	Any	500 µV/m @ 3 m	A	15.209
22.01-23.12 GHz	SPURIOUS EMISSIONS ONLY	500 µV/m @ 3 m with higher emissions permitted according to Section 15.205(d)	A	15.205
23.12-23.6 GHz	Intermittent Control Signals	12,500 µV/m @ 3 m	A	15.231
	Periodic Transmissions	5,000 µV/m @ 3 m	A	15.231
	Any	500 µV/m @ 3 m	A	15.209
23.6-24 GHz	SPURIOUS EMISSIONS ONLY	500 µV/m @ 3 m with higher emissions permitted according to Section 15.205(d)	A	15.205
24-24.075 GHz	Any	250,000 µV/m @ 3 m	A	15.249
24.075-24.175 GHz	Field Disturbance Sensors	2,500,000 µV/m @ 3 m	A	15.245
	Any	250,000 µV/m @ 3 m	A	15.249
24.175-24.25 GHz	Any	250,000 µV/m @ 3 m	A	15.249
24.25-31.2 GHz	Intermittent Control Signals	12,500 µV/m @ 3 m	A	15.231
	Periodic Transmissions	5,000 µV/m @ 3 m	A	15.231
	Any	500 µV/m @ 3 m	A	15.209
31.2-31.8 GHz	SPURIOUS EMISSIONS ONLY	500 µV/m @ 3 m with higher emissions permitted according to Section 15.205(d)	A	15.205
31.8-36.43 GHz	Intermittent Control Signals	12,500 µV/m @ 3 m	A	15.231
31.8-36.43 GHz (cont.)	Periodic Transmissions	5,000 µV/m @ 3 m	A	15.231
	Any	500 µV/m @ 3 m	A	15.209
36.43-36.5 GHz	SPURIOUS EMISSIONS ONLY	500 µV/m @ 3 m with higher emissions permitted according to Section 15.205(d)	A	15.205

36.5-38.6 GHz	Intermittent Control Signals	12,500 µV/m @ 3 m	A	15.231
	Periodic Transmissions	5,000 µV/m @ 3 m	A	15.231
	Any	500 µV/m @ 3 m	A	15.209
Above 38.6 GHz	SPURIOUS EMISSIONS ONLY	500 µV/m @ 3 m with higher emissions permitted according to Section 15.205(d)	A	15.205

Cordless telephones

Cordless telephones are required to incorporate circuitry that uses digital security codes to help prevent the phone from unintentionally connecting to the public switched telephone network when it encounters radio frequency noise from another cordless phone or from some other source. Cordless phones that do not have this circuitry (phones that were manufactured or imported prior to September 11, 1991) are required to have a statement on the package in which they are sold that warns of the danger of unintentional line seizures and indicates what features the packaged phone has to help prevent them.

Section 15.214

The preceding table describes the frequencies that cordless phones can use.

Tunnel radio systems

Many tunnels have naturally surrounding earth and/or water that attenuates radio waves. Transmitters that are operated inside these tunnels are not subject to any radiation limits inside the tunnel. Instead, the signals they produce must meet the Part 15 general radiated emission limits on the outside of the tunnel, including its openings. They also must comply with the conducted emission limits on the electric power lines outside of the tunnel.

Section 15.211

Buildings and other structures that are not surrounded by earth or water (e.g. oil storage tanks) are not tunnels. Transmitters that are operated inside such structures are subject to the same standards as transmitters operated in an open area.

Commonly Asked Questions

What happens if one sells, imports or uses non-compliant low-power transmitters?

The FCC rules are designed to control the marketing of low-power transmitters and, to a lesser extent, their use. If the operation of a non-compliant transmitter causes interference to authorized radio communications, the user should stop operating the transmitter or correct the problem causing the interference. However, the person (or company) that sold this non-compliant transmitter to the user has violated the FCC marketing rules in Part 2 as well as federal law. The act of selling or leasing, offering to sell or lease, or importing a low-power transmitter that has not gone through the appropriate FCC equipment authorization procedure is a violation of the Commission's rules and federal law. Violators may be subject to an enforcement action by the Commission's Field Operations Bureau that could result in:

Section 15.1

Section 15.5

Section 2.803
Section 2.805
Section 2.1203

- o forfeiture of all non-compliant equipment
- o $100,000/$200,000 criminal penalty for an individual/organization
- o a criminal fine totalling twice the gross gain obtained from sales of the non-compliant equipment
- o an administrative fine totalling $10,000/day per violation, up to a maximum of $75,000

Section 1.80
47 U.S.C. 302
47 U.S.C. 501
47 U.S.C. 502
47 U.S.C. 503
47 U.S.C. 510
18 U.S.C. 3571

What changes can be made to an FCC-authorized device without requiring a new FCC authorization?

The person or company that obtained FCC authorization for a Part 15 transmitter is permitted to make the following types of changes:

For **certified equipment,** the holder of the grant of certification, or the holder's agent, can make minor modifications to the circuitry, appearance or other design aspects of the transmitter. Minor modifications are divided into two categories: Class I permissive changes and Class II permissive changes. Major changes are not permitted.

Section 2.929
Section 2.1043

> Minor changes that do not increase the radio frequency emissions from the transmitter do not require the grantee to file any information with the FCC. These are called *Class I permissive changes*. (Note: if a Class I permissive change results in a product that looks different than the one that was certified it is strongly suggested that photos of the modified transmitter be filed with the FCC.)

> Minor changes that increase the radio frequency emissions from the transmitter require the grantee to file complete information about the change along with results of tests showing that the equipment continues to comply with FCC technical standards. In this case, the modified equipment may not be marketed under the existing grant of certification prior to acknowledgement by the Commission that the change is acceptable. These are called *Class II permissive changes*.

> Major changes require that a new grant be obtained by submitting a new application with complete test results. Some examples of major changes include: changes to the basic frequency determining and stabilizing circuitry; changes to the frequency multiplication stages or basic modulator circuit; and, major changes to the size, shape or shielding properties of the case.

No changes are permitted to certified equipment by anyone other than the grantee or the grantee's designated agent; except, however, that changes to the FCC ID without any other changes to the equipment may be performed by anyone by filing an abbreviated application.

Section 2.1043
Section 2.933

For **verified equipment**, any changes may be made to the circuitry, appearance or other design aspects of the device as long as the manufacturer (importer, if the equipment is imported) has on file updated circuit drawings and test data showing that the equipment continues to comply with the FCC rules.

Section 2.952
Section 2.953
Section 2.955

What is the relationship between "microvolts per meter" and Watts?

Watts are the units used to describe the amount of power generated by a transmitter. Microvolts per meter (μV/m) are the units used to describe the strength of an electric field created by the operation of a transmitter.

A particular transmitter that generates a constant level of power (Watts) can produce electric fields of different strengths (μV/m) depending on, among other things, the type of transmission line and antenna connected to it. Because it is the electric field that causes interference to authorized radio communications, and since a particular electric field strength does not directly correspond to a particular level of transmitter power, most of the Part 15 emission limits are specified in field strength.

Although the precise relationship between power and field strength can depend on a number of additional factors, a commonly-used equation to approximate their relationship is:

$$\frac{PG}{4\pi D^2} = \frac{E^2}{120\pi}$$

where: P is transmitter power in Watts;
    G is the numerical gain of the transmitting antenna relative to an isotropic source;
    D is the distance of the measuring point from the electrical center of the antenna in meters; and,
    E is field strength in volts/meter.

$4\pi D^2$ is the surface area of the sphere centered at the radiating source whose surface is D meters from the radiating source. 120π is the characteristic impedance of free space in ohms.

Using this equation, and assuming a unity gain antenna (G = 1) and a measurement distance of 3 meters (D = 3), a formula for determining power given field strength can be developed:

$$P = 0.3E^2$$

where: P is the transmitter power (EIRP) in watts and E is the field strength in volts/meter.

Additional Information

Obtaining rules

The FCC rules are contained in *Title 47 of the Code of Federal Regulations* (47 CFR). Parts 2 and 15 are applicable to low-power transmitters. Part 68 applies, in addition, to equipment that connects to the public switched telephone network. To obtain a copy of these rules contact:

Superintendent of Documents
U.S. Government Printing Office
P.O. Box 371954
Pittsburgh, PA 15250-7954

Tel: (202) 512-1800 / Fax: (202) 512-2250
(8 AM - 5 PM Eastern Time)
(GPO deposit accounts, VISA and MasterCard accepted)

Obtaining forms and fee filing guides

To obtain copies of FCC Form 159 ("Fee Advice Form"), FCC Form 731 ("Application for Equipment Authorization") FCC Form 730 ("Registration of Telephone and Data Terminal Equipment"), and fee filing guides contact:

Federal Communications Commission
Forms Distribution Center
9300 E. Hampton Drive
Capitol Heights, MD 20743
Tel: (202) 418-3676 or 1-800 418-3676

Equipment authorization procedures

Questions regarding equipment authorization procedures for Part 15 transmitters should be addressed to:

Federal Communications Commission
Equipment Authorization Division
Application Processing Branch, MS 1300F1
7435 Oakland Mills Road
Columbia, MD 21046
Tel: (301) 725-1585 / Fax: (301) 344-2050
E-Mail: labinfo@fcc.gov

Obtaining equipment authorization filing packets

Application packets to assist applicants in applying for certification of transmitters and obtaining a grantee code are available from:

Federal Communications Commission
Equipment Authorization Division
Customer Service Branch
Tel: (301) 725-1585, Ext 639 / Fax: (301) 344-2050
E-Mail: labinfo@fcc.gov

Rule interpretations

Questions regarding interpretations of the Part 2 and Part 15 rules as they apply to low-power transmitters and measurement procedures used to test these transmitters for compliance with the Part 15 technical standards, should be addressed to:

Federal Communications Commission
Equipment Authorization Division
Customer Service Branch, MS 1300F2
7435 Oakland Mills Road
Columbia, MD 21046
Tel: (301) 725-1585 / Fax: (301) 344-2050
E-Mail: labinfo@fcc.gov

Part 68 registration requirements

Questions regarding the Part 68 rules as they apply to equipment that connects to the public switched telephone network (cordless phones, wireless modems etc.) should be addressed to:

Federal Communications Commission
Network Services Division, MS 1600B
Washington, DC 20554
Tel: (202) 418-2342 / Fax: (202) 418-2345

Experimental licenses

Prior to obtaining FCC equipment authorization, Part 15 transmitters may not be operated without an experimental license; *except*, however, that no license is needed to test a Part 15 transmitter for compliance with the FCC rules. Information on obtaining an experimental license may be obtained from:

Federal Communications Commission
New Technology Development Division
Experimental Licensing Branch, MS 1300E1
Washington, DC 20554
Tel: (202) 418-2479 / Fax: (202) 418-1918

FCC's computer bulletin board

The FCC maintains a computer bulletin board, called the Public Access Link (PAL), that contains information about the FCC rules, proposed or recent rule changes, application procedures, fees and equipment authorizations. Applicants may check on the status of their applications, and others may check the validity of an FCC ID on a piece of equipment, by dialing this bulletin board via computer modem at:

(301) 725-1072
Modem set up: 8 bits, no parity, 1 stop bit
(parity is ignored on input and system does not send parity on output)

Status desk

Applicants who do not have access to a computer may check on the status of their applications by calling the Equipment Authorization Division's status desk at:

(301) 725-1585, Ext. 300 (Monday-Thursday, 2:00 - 4:30 PM)

www.ingramcontent.com/pod-product-compliance
Lightning Source LLC
Chambersburg PA
CBHW080624180526
45168CB00007B/3044